How to Analyze People

Dark Psychology

Dark Secrets to Analyze and Influence Anyone Using Body Language, Human Psychology, Subliminal Persuasion and NLP

By

James W. Williams

© Copyright 2018
All rights reserved.

The content contained within this book may not be reproduced, duplicated or transmitted without direct written permission from the author or the publisher.

Under no circumstances will any blame or legal responsibility be held against the publisher, or author, for any damages, reparation, or monetary loss due to the information contained within this book. Either directly or indirectly.

Legal Notice:

This book is copyright protected. This book is only for personal use. You cannot amend, distribute, sell, use, quote or paraphrase any part, or the content within this book, without the consent of the author or publisher.

James W. Williams

<u>Disclaimer Notice:</u>

Please note the information contained within this document is for educational and entertainment purposes only. All effort has been executed to present accurate, up to date, and reliable, complete information. No warranties of any kind are declared or implied. Readers acknowledge that the author is not engaging in the rendering of legal, financial, medical or professional advice. The content within this book has been derived from various sources. Please consult a licensed professional before attempting any techniques outlined in this book.

By reading this document, the reader agrees that under no circumstances is the author responsible for any losses, direct or indirect, which are incurred as a result of the use of information contained within this document, including, but not limited to, — errors, omissions, or inaccuracies.

Table Of Contents

Introduction 8

Chapter 1 – Body Language 10

    Cultural Differences 11

Studying Others' Movements 12

    Eye Contact 15

    Mouth Movements 16

    Nodding 18

    Hands and Arms 20

Signals 22

    Starting a Conversation 23

    Leading the Conversation 24

How Your Body Language Affects You 26

    Open Your Mind 28

    Improve Your Memory 29

Verbal Cues 30

    Emphasis Cues 33

    Organizational Cues 34

    Watch Your Pitch 35

    Listen to Others 38

    Apologizing 41

The Power of Your Body 43
Smiling is Important 45

Chapter 2 – Human Psychology 47

Creating Vulnerability 49
Ask for Help 51
Ask for More 53

Making Connections 54
Use their Name 57
Mirroring Behavior 58
Flattery gets you everywhere 60

The Power of Words 61

Psychological Theories 64
Priming...66
Amplification Hypothesis..68
The Scarcity Effect 70

Chapter 3 – Subliminal Persuasion 72
It's Not about Manipulation..73

Confidence is Key 74
Body Language Techniques 75
Keep Speech Clear 76

Framing Conversations 77
Choose Positivity 78
Plan Your Outcome 80

Physical Persuasion 81
- Choosing What to Wear 82
- Scent is Important 83

NLP Tactics 84
- Switching Up Physiology 85
- Visualization 86
- Taking Away the Ability to Say No 87

Conclusion 88
Thank you! 90

Your Free Gift

As a way of saying thanks for your purchase, I wanted to offer you a free bonus E-book called *"Bulletproof Confidence Checklist: Eliminate Limiting Beliefs, Overcome Shyness and Social Anxiety and Achieve Your Goals"*.

In this guide, you will discover:

- What is shyness & social anxiety and the psychology behind it
- Simple treatments for social anxiety
- Breakdown of the traits of a confident person
- Breakdown of the traits of a socially awkward person
- Easy, actionable tips for overcoming being socially awkward
- Confidence checklist to ensure you're on the right path of self-development

To grab your free bonus book just go to:

- https://theartofmastery.com/confidence/

Introduction

In my book *Persuasion,* the different ways that we have been persuaded were touched on. Many of us might have gone a long time in our lives without even realizing that we had been persuaded and manipulated so often. The damages of this manipulation can last forever, and it can be hard to recover. Once you become aware of how others might be subliminally persuading you, you can better protect yourself from these tactics in the future to maintain your independence and stay out of others' influence.

It's important to remember that by understanding these concepts you're better equipped to identify and defend against them, and your new knowledge shouldn't be about how you can use those same tactics to manipulate other people. There is a difference between evil manipulation and trying to convince someone of something else. You don't want to trick someone into doing things for you when they won't get any benefit at all. You only want to use these tactics when you need to persuade someone for something and you can't blatantly ask them for help. There are people that are harder to convince than others, so you might need to use some strategies of persuasion.

Who might you need to persuade? You never want to take advantage of someone that already doesn't have much to give. Those you should be trying to persuade are people that hold power. You might want to learn how to convince your boss to get a raise. Maybe you want to try to get your girlfriend to move in with you. Perhaps you have to ask your parents for a loan. You don't want to "punch down," but instead, "reach up."

This book will start with how you can analyze other people. Once you have a better understanding of how to analyze those around you both physically and psychologically, you'll be able to persuade them better towards your favor.

Chapter 1 – Body Language

One of the easiest ways to analyze other people is to look at their body language. How a person holds themselves, moves, and even speaks can tell you a lot about them. Everyone has plenty of variation between their mannerisms, and there's no exact way to tell what makes up a person. There are still many similar indications among groups of people that can give you a deep insight into how someone functions.

It's not easy because it starts with becoming aware of your own body language. In order to understand and attempt to overcome the enigma that is body language, you have to be hyper aware. In book one, we took you through the process of becoming aware of your thoughts and where they might come from. Now it's time to work on becoming aware of your body. In order to learn what makes a person different from others based on their body language, you have to first look at yourself and analyze how you hold your body.

Some people might be more aware of their movements than they are their thoughts. Women are likely going to be more aware of their bodies and the space they take up, mostly because of the patriarchal society we grew up in. Everyone still might find difficulty in confronting the way they hold their body. You can lose focus while trying to maintain awareness, becoming too insecure with your own body and movements.

This first chapter will go into the basics of body language while also laying a basis for how you can analyze others. Once you get to know the body movements better of another person, you can also understand what makes them unique. The more you know about a person, the better you can conclude the best strategy for persuasion.

Cultural Differences

Every person is different, and sometimes, how one person holds their body has a different meaning than someone who stands the same way.

There are plenty of ways that a person's body language differs, so it's important to remember that not everything about a certain body movement is 100% true for every person. This is especially important to remember when talking to people with different cultural backgrounds.

There are some cultures that practice modesty, so touching might be completely off limits. Other cultures might be more open to expressing their feelings through their bodies, so culture is important to remember when thinking about how a person might use their body.

Studying Others' Movements

Once you become more aware of body movements and what they might represent, you can start studying them when interacting with different people. Everyone you come in contact with uses their body to represent different things. Some people are closed off, and others might be more open. These are some small differences you could tell just by observing someone's body language.

When studying other people and yourself, it's important to try and act naturally as well. It can be easy to become hyper-aware of your movements but know that you don't have to hold your body a certain way. Not everyone is as aware of body movements as others might be, so at the end of the day, don't look into your own movements too much.

Still, once you start studying others' body movements, you'll start to realize how much you can get to know them. Certain things might all start to make sense after meeting a variety of individuals. You might notice that one of your friends is rather pretentious in the way they hold themselves or talk. Other friends might show how insecure they are with themselves, even though you thought they had been incredibly confident since you'd known them.

Knowing a person's body language and having insight as to why they might move a certain way can allow you to understand them at their core better. This gives you better leverage when it comes to persuading them. You might want to match the confidence of your boss when striking up a deal for a raise. Perhaps you noticed you need to be more relaxed around certain friends that seem to be shy or nervous. Becoming aware of your body language can be scary at first, but eventually, you'll be comfortable with the way you move.

To start practicing being comfortable with your own body, try hanging out in front of a mirror. When you're eating dinner, watching TV, or even lounging in bed, set up a mirror so you can see how you hold yourself. Once you get an outsider's perspective on how you move, you'll be able to see how others move as well.

Eye Contact

Eye contact is one of the biggest clues you can use to determine how someone truly is. It's important to become aware of your own use of eye contact as well, because it gives others clues about your personality and true nature. Maintaining eye contact is important to let a person know that you're interested in what they're saying and that they have your full attention.

It can also be overused, however, and let people know that you're trying too hard to convince them that you're listening. Too much eye contact can sometimes intimidate others as well, so if you notice that a person is getting nervous because of the amount of eye contact you're having with them, change it up every now and then.

Pupil dilation can be a direct indication that a person is interested in what you're saying. Studies have proven that when a person's pupils begin dilating whom you're making eye contact with, they are more interested in what you have to say. They are listening to you with their utmost attention, and they're thinking deeply about what you're saying. You know when a person's pupils are dilated while talking to you that they are legitimately interested in the conversation.

Shifty eyes will indicate the opposite. Someone who is looking at your eyes back and forth is probably trying to convince you that they are listening. They are aware that they need to try and make eye contact, but they are completely zoned out with what you are saying. Those with shifty eyes might also be lying to you or trying to deceit you in some way. They might be having difficulty maintaining eye contact with you because they know they are being deceitful.

Mouth Movements

What someone does with their mouth is very crucial in understanding their personality as well. Someone with tight or pursed lips might be trying to concentrate, or they also might be trying hard to hide a sour face. You can analyze a person's smile as well. If the corners of their eyes aren't creased, they might be forcing a smile with you.

Someone that's faking a smile isn't necessarily evil, they might just be thinking of something else, too distracted to give their full attention to what you're saying. Sometimes, smiles are also reactions to uncomfortable situations.

When monkeys smile, it's not because they are happy, but mostly because they are showing their teeth as a way of threatening those around them. When they feel scared and nervous, they'll open their mouths wide, showing that they have teeth they could use to hurt. The same goes for dogs. They only show their teeth when they are feeling threatened. For humans, this can be true sometimes as well, but on a subconscious level.

Nervous laughing and smiling are just a way for a person to alleviate their tension. You can tell someone is genuinely smiling when they have creases in the corners of their eyes.

A person that is continually covering their mouth also is usually nervous. They might bite their lip, finger, or put a fist over their mouth. Knowing when a person is uncomfortable or nervous can sometimes be helpful when trying to persuade them. We'll discuss how and when to use this knowledge to persuade others in the next two chapters.

Nodding

How a person turns and tilts their head can be a subtle movement. Most of the time, others aren't as aware when they are moving their head around. The neck and head movements of the person you're talking to can give you great insight into what they might be thinking on a deeper level.

Someone that nods their head rather quickly while listening to you might just be anxious, trying to move the conversation along as quick as possible. They're attempting to set a pace for you so that you speak faster. They want to let you know they hear you, but you're not speaking fast enough. If someone is doing this to you, try to speed up your words in order to hold their attention.

Someone who tilts their head to the side might have a legitimate interest in what you're saying. They are attempting to turn an ear towards you, so they can hear you better, whether they're aware of their movements or not. They also are indicating to you that they hear you and they want you to keep talking. It's a way for them to get closer to you in the conversation without having to make any interjections or interruptions.

If someone is nodding too artificially, they might just be attempting to convince you that they are interested in what you are saying. They could be aware that they should be paying attention, but they might have lost interest. In an attempt to keep up, they pretend to nod their head. They also might not understand what you're saying, so they nod to make you think they're keeping up. If you notice others around you are artificially nodding their head, it'd be worth it to either change the subject to regain attention or explain yourself better as they might just be confused.

Mimicking someone's head movements can be very helpful in using persuasion. A gentle tilt of the head while listening to them can show that you are comprehending what they're saying. It can also show that you're empathetic to them, especially if they seem to be talking about something that is hard for them.

Hands and Arms

How someone uses their hands and arms is another way that body language can be interpreted to get a better understanding of the people you're interacting with. Our hands represent so much about ourselves. They're a way of expressing out stories, putting different emphasis on various parts. If someone's telling a story, they're going to use hand gestures to keep people interested. Think of someone engaged in a conversation as someone that's directing an orchestra. They'll lift their hands to keep up a rhythm and pace for those listening around.

Someone's hands and arms can also express how open or closed off they are. They can be like the doorway into someone's body. If they're crossed tightly in front of someone's chest, that person might be a little more closed off, not wanting to engage too much in conversation. Having their arms crossed doesn't always mean that someone is necessarily closed off. They might also just be wanting to rest their arms, so if they're loosely hanging in front of their chest, they're likely just casually listening to you.

Someone that has their arms outstretched, maybe over their head, will likely be very open and possibly even trying to exert power over a situation. Someone with their hands on their hips might also be trying to assert their power.

Signals

Everyone has different body language ques that they use as signals. Between cultures, genders, and ages, different movements someone makes with their bodies can be conscious or subconscious signals that they're giving to the people around them. Signals let other people know bits of information without having to say anything at all.

Someone with their arms crossed, eyes fading on a couch at a party is giving the signal that they're likely ready to head home for the night. Someone else on that couch could be sitting on the edge of their seat, laughing loudly, signaling they're not going to be heading to bed anytime soon.

Signals help the people around the signaler know things that they might not easily be able to express with their bodies. Some are very good at picking up on other people's signals, and some people struggle to understand those around them.

When it comes to trying to persuade someone, there are some crucial signals that a person will need to be able to properly lead a conversation.

Starting a Conversation

Next time you're sitting quietly in a room with another person, wait until they start the conversation to speak. This will allow you to study how they might start a conversation. Most people will give some sort of signal with their body that they are about to begin speaking. They might clear their throat, turn their head, adjust their shirt, or shift in their seat. There is usually something, no matter how small it might be, that a person does right before they start a conversation.

When it comes to your turn to start a conversation, notice what you do before you begin speaking. Don't start with an "um," or "uh." That lets the other person know right away that you're not very sure about what you're going to say. Try starting a conversation without doing anything.

See if you can just start speaking without clearing your throat, moving your head, or doing anything else. Study how the other person reacts. They might be surprised or thrown off guard that one of you had started speaking.

Starting a conversation, especially one that is meant to persuade another person, is important for laying the groundwork for your argument. No one is going to want to give their full attention to someone that is struggling to start. If you're nervous and jumping over your words right off the bat, it's going to be much harder to keep up.

Leading the Conversation

Once the conversation has started, it can be tricky to maintain the right amount of back and forth. You don't want to be too pushy, but you also don't want to let them talk too much, not allowing you anytime to state your points. If you feel as though the other person isn't letting you talk enough, there are obvious phrases you can use to speak your mind. You might try saying something like, "can I just say...," "could I speak for a minute?" or "I'm listening but can I say something really quick?"

These can be hard to say in some situations, and some people might even perceive you as being rude if you make a large interjection. What your best option might be is to use your body to redirect focus. Put your hands on your hips or tilt your head to let the other person know that you have something to say. Try leaning in to let them know that you want to take over as the leader of your current conversation.

Leading the conversation can be tricky, because no one wants to listen to someone that is interrupting them. It's still important that you get your turn to speak as well. There are ways you can practice leading conversations so that when it comes time to have an important persuasion, you can properly lead. Next time you want to say something, don't. Instead let the other person continue speaking and interject later. Sometimes we get so anxious to say our part we distract from the true conversation, invalidating any argument we have to the person that we interrupted.

An alternative way to practice leading the conversation is to speak up the next time you want to say something. If you have something to say but you would rather just keep quiet, force yourself to say what you want. These two methods of practice will give you two alternate perspectives on leading a conversation that you might not get otherwise.

How Your Body Language Affects You

Believe it or not, how you use your body can directly affect how you function as well. There are ways that you can use to improve how you think, and the capacity of your memory just by the way that you use your hands and arms. Not only are there physical differences in terms of how you use your body, but you will also be affected by the way others perceive you.

If you're constantly closed off, always crossing your arms, there are probably a lot of people that might not open up or talk to you because they assume you have no interest in conversation. If you're always very open with your body, exerting confidence and holding yourself high, others might end up being intimidated by you. You might not have any intention of closing others off or being intimidating, but your body can show that in ways that your mouth doesn't.

It can be tricky to become self-aware of your body movements, but once you do, you can really alter what someone thinks of you. There are some people that might have a strong conscious mind, but perhaps they hate their body. They then might close others off by trying to hide their bodies, making others think that they're judgmental. Sometimes, a person is just trying to cover up their body and not themselves. You would be surprised at how much confidence you can feel just by changing up the way you hold your body. People can still see what you look like even if you keep your arms crossed. You might think you're altering other's perceptions of you, but really, you're just remaining closed off.

There are other ways that your own body language can actually mentally affect you.

Open Your Mind

Someone that starts opening their arms when they talk will begin to let others know that they are much more open-minded. If you stand with arms open, or just hanging relaxed by your side, you let the people around you know that you are confident and willing to talk with them about different things.

While having open arms is a signal for others, it's also a signal for your brain. Studies show that by standing with open arms verses crossed ones, you can actually signal your brain to be more open.

You'll start to think of new ideas that you wouldn't if you kept your arms crossed. The same goes for the rest of your body. The more open you are with your movements, the more you allow your brain to have different ideas.

Improve Your Memory

Those that talk with their hands also tend to have a better memory than those that don't. Using your hands can put physical reminders in your brain for ideas and thoughts that you might be discussing. If you mimic numbers or shapes when you're talking about different ideas, especially in a business setting, not only will you remember what you're discussing better, but those around you will find your story more memorable as well.

Using your hands to talk while telling a story will also help you remember the things that you went through. You're encouraging your brain to continue thinking, and keeping your arms open, just as we mentioned in the last section, will open up your brain to new thoughts and feelings you might not have had should you have spoken with your arms crossed and closed off.

Verbal Cues

While there are many things that a person can say with their body, there are many more things that they can say with their mouth. There's a seemingly limitless amount of languages out there, as each specific language has many subparts. Think of how many different accents there might be in just New York City. As we continue to develop and blend different cultures and languages, only more will develop. It's hard enough to keep up with what we already know, but there are ways to still pick up on others' meaning without having to memorize every word in the dictionary.

Just because a person says a certain word doesn't

indicate that they're actually meaning what they say. How many times have you said you were "fine," when really, you wanted to explode with thoughts? We say what we don't mean all the time because it isn't always easy to put words to our thoughts and feelings. Many people take their frustration or sadness out on other people when they don't actually mean anything that they're saying.

Knowing why people say the things they do can be one of the trickiest codes to try and crack. You don't always have to know exactly what a person means in order to understand what they're trying to say. You can pick up on what a person's intention is by listening to how they talk and mixing that with their body language. It's important to read someone's mood so you don't say the wrong thing or anything that could potentially change the direction of the conversation.

Next time you find something on TV that's in a different language than any you can speak, try watching without subtitles. You'll be surprised to see that you actually understand part of the storyline. Don't look at what they're saying, but how they're saying it. Is there pain in their eyes? Do they look happy or sad? Sometimes if you can't understand what a person is saying, maybe because the room is loud or they're speaking softly, try looking into their eyes. You might get a better sense of what they're saying than if you just watch the words their mouth is attempting to put together.

There are certain specific cues that someone can give when they're trying to direct a conversation. When you're trying to persuade someone, you might want to try and use different keywords to help you in leading the conversation. Some people get too hung up on the actual words someone is saying when they should just be trying to listen to the message they're getting across.

It can seem difficult to try to crack what someone else means, but it can be done. Think about your pets. You can tell if your dog is sad, sleepy, hungry, or in a playful mood, but you don't have actual conversations with them. Sometimes you can analyze what a person is saying best by figuring out the noises they're making rather than dissecting every word that they say.

Emphasis Cues

When trying to persuade someone, you're going to want to have a pretty good argument already prepared in order to build your case. You might want to include some emphasis cues when you're speaking. It can be hard to incorporate these phrases naturally, but it's good to practice so you can become a better persuader.

"This is important," "you need to know," "let me explain," are all phrases that grab the attention of the person that you're speaking too. You might start to notice others' emphasis cues better after reading this section as well. You should be listening, and using in your own speech, phrases that seem to put emphasis on an important part of a conversation.

Sometimes, these emphasis cues aren't even actual phrases. They might just be verbal indications that something is important, such as someone raising their voice when talking about an important part of their argument. They also might repeat the word several times or stop for a pause in order for the listener to take in what they just said. Emphasis cues are important to understand in order to get a better grasp of what might be important to an individual. If you listen to what they're putting emphasis on, you'll be able to also formulate your thoughts and arguments around the things that are important to them.

Organizational Cues

"First, second, third," "to summarize," "the topic is," are all phrases that could be considered organizational cues. These cues help a person indicate that they are trying to organize their thoughts, again, maybe putting emphasis on the things that are the most important.

Organizational cues are important for you to use in your arguments in persuasions in order to get people on your side. You want them to know that you're listening to what they have to say, and that they should be listening to you. You're trying to formulate a plan based on both your thoughts and opinions, and not just the words of one specific individual.

Organizational cues allow the speaker to put emphasis on what's important while also maintaining a clear thought and direct focus. Organizational cues might not be phrases either. It could just be someone clearing their throat, redirecting the conversation back to a previous topic, or stopping in order for everyone to collect their thoughts.

Watch Your Pitch

Pitch is an important key when trying to direct

one's conversation in their favor. Pitch is the level of your voice, and the overall sound quality. Someone with a deep pitch might have a more soothing tone, while someone with a high-pitched voice might make their listeners more alert. Not everyone can help the natural pitch of their voice. There are some people that have extremely low voices that are hard to hear, and some people just have naturally shrill voices that seem as though they bother everyone around them!

While your natural pitch can't always be controlled, you can at least help direct that pitch towards a more productive tone in order to keep your listeners engaged with what you have to say. Many of us let our pitch become too high and whiny when we are in professional settings, trying to keep our dictation sharp. If you feel like your voice is becoming high and shrill, don't be afraid to stop, clear your throat, and start again. The people around you will likely be grateful that you're adjusting your tone for their listening pleasure.

Be careful not to let the end of your voice go up when speaking. Many people, especially when talking on a phone, tend to let the end of their words go up like they're asking a question. This kind of speaking is also common among those that might be giving a speech. They'll say a phrase very clearly with dictation, but they'll also end the sentence in a high pitched way as if they're asking a question. This is something that should be avoided in order to keep the attention of your listeners.

It's important to find your optimal pitch. Some people have very soft voices that can be hard to hear. If this is the case, it's important to practice speaking up when it's necessary. Someone that tends to speak loudly should try talking low as often as possible to help balance their pitch out. The greatest way to practice is alone, and if you record what you're saying. You don't want to deeply analyze the way you speak too much, but practicing always helps, especially for those that find difficulty in speaking their voice.

It's also important to have a confident pitch to let others know they should listen to you. Someone that's always talking timidly or like they're asking a question will let the others around them know that what they have to say isn't interesting. If you're so unsure of what you're saying, why should someone else listen to you? The best way to ensure others are paying attention is to make sure that you speak with confidence.

Listen to Others

Talking about yourself can elicit the same good feelings that money and food cause. People like talking about themselves more than they enjoy listening to other people talk about themselves for the most part. While it can seem selfish, it's true that most people would prefer to talk about themselves. This means that when conversing with other people, you should avoid talking about yourself too much.

You don't want to make the conversation

completely about other people, but no one will pay attention if the only thing you talk about is yourself. Giving advice can also be helpful, but people generally don't engage as often with those that offer too much advice, especially when it isn't asked for.

Listening to other people can actually be challenging for some. They might find it difficult to not let their mind wander, especially if the other person is talking too much about themselves. Some people will find that they're usually forming their next thought while the other person is talking instead of actually listening to them. If you find your mind wandering when someone else is talking, redirect your thoughts back to their words. Don't just listen to what they're saying. Watch how they're saying it. Listen to their voice and look into their eyes. People will notice whether or not you're listening to them. Even if they aren't skilled in body language, they will still be able to at least sense that you might not be fully engaged as well.

Don't just put an emphasis on listening to others. Make the conversation about them as well. Ask questions about the person, attempting to get to know them better. You'll find that people usually like to answer questions about themselves. This is often a technique you'll see in many salespeople. They'll ask where you got your shirt, or if you've had a good day. This is to get the person thinking about themselves, and they'll usually end up opening up a bit more to the salesperson as well.

People don't like to be corrected. While it can be hard to avoid sometimes, most people don't want to be interrupted to be told that they were wrong. Most people will respect you much more if you just let them talk rather than trying to prove them wrong. This is very important to remember, especially when trying to persuade and analyze others.

Talk about "we," not "you." If you're trying to make suggestions, maybe to a spouse or friend about an improvement in their lifestyle, use "we" instead. Don't say, "you should try waking up earlier on the weekends," say, "we should get up early on Sunday and go on a walk together!" People will respond much better to suggestions if you include yourself.

Apologizing

It can be hard to apologize, especially for those with high levels of pride, but it's important in gaining the respect of the people around you. If you apologize for being late rather than giving every explanation you can, most will respond much better to this than if you were to try to make yourself look better with excuses.

They also like to see humility, and that you maybe aren't afraid to express yourself. If you can open up with someone and just say, "I'm sorry I didn't respond to your text, I was just having a really bad day," they'll usually be very forgiving rather than if you would've just blown them off.

However, don't apologize too much. It can lead

others to not trust you. Sometimes we have the urge to apologize for things that were out of our control in an attempt to make ourselves look better. We'll say, "I'm sorry the movie was so bad!" after going out for a movie night, even though we had no control over the production. This is nice every once in a while, and certainly shows humility and vulnerability to those around you. But too much of it can also make you seem untrustworthy to others.

If you have to apologize after every little thing you say, why should anyone listen to you in the first place? Next time you feel the urge to apologize for something that was out of your control, try saying thank you instead. After having a long conversation with a friend, don't say, "Sorry you had to listen to me rant!" Instead, try something like, "Thank you for being such a great listener. I'm glad to have a friend like you!" People will generally respond much more positively to a thankful person than someone that always invalidates themselves. You'll find that you start to treat yourself much better if you stick to this method of apology as well.

The Power of Your Body

Our bodies have so much power, and not just with how much we're able to lift or carry. Physical strength is important, but even the weakest of people have the ability to control a room with their body movements alone. At this point in the book, you should have a basic understanding of what a person's body language might mean.

We can't get into every specific detail of what someone's physical actions might be trying to convey, but the framework for how to analyze those movements is there. Once you understand how someone else might be using their body to persuade others, you can start to work on your own skills of persuasion.

There are many ways that someone can use their

body to convince others to do what they want, but it won't always work on everyone. Some people respond to sexual persuasion while others are repulsed by the thought. Some people respond to a physical threat from those that seem stronger than them, but others might be ready for the fight.

There are plenty of ways that you can use your body to persuade others without being sexual or physically intimidating. Keeping your body open and visible is crucial in letting others know they can trust you. Try making sure to remove physical barriers that might keep you separated from the person you're talking to. Step around a chair or table that's blocking you from making a full connection with the person you're trying to talk to.

This also shows that you're confident and interested in speaking your mind while hearing what the other person has to say as well. When analyzing other people's movements, you can also figure out what things you can do yourself to be more confident. Study certain celebrities and see how they hold themselves in various scenarios. Everyone has their own movements, but mimicking others can still help you find your own footing when it comes to having a persuasive demeanor overall.

Smiling is Important

Our smiles are one of the most powerful tools we've been given. You can turn any situation from bad to good just by turning up the corners of your mouth. Some people feel as though if they don't have straight teeth or smiles that are bright white, they aren't worth anything. Even those that don't have all their teeth can have much more beautiful smiles than someone that's spent thousands on dental work.

A smile isn't just about what teeth you're showing. It's a way to engage another person. Studies have proven that most people will smile if someone else smiles at them first. If they do smile, they'll end up having a better mood overall. It can seem weird, but simply smiling can lift someone's spirits. Next time you are feeling particularly down, smile. It sounds so silly, but it might work. Smile over and over again, and even though it might not turn your mood around, it will certainly help to at least temporarily lift your spirits.

Chapter 2 – Human Psychology

You don't have to be a psychology expert to have a basic understanding of how the human brain works. Once you get to know how our brains operate, you can begin to analyze people much more easily. You'll start to realize that those around might act a certain way because of the way they were raised and the things that they were taught. Once you have a basic understanding of human psychology, you'll start to put together the pieces of what makes the people around you the unique individuals they are. You'll realize a lot more makes sense about why a person does the things they do if you can look into their psychology.

Even those incredibly skilled in human psychology make mistakes every now and then. There is still so little known about the human brain that of course, not everyone is going to be right all the time. The brain is the most complex organ in the body of any animal, not just humans. It can be hard to understand it and figure out what secrets lie inside that make a person tick. You can still attempt to get to know the inner workings of a person's brain, and even though you won't have all the answers, you'll start to understand them a little better.

There is little known about the human brain, and what is known has been discovered by the brain itself! Isn't it strange to think that everything we know about the brain was taught to us by our own brains? This complex organ will never fully make sense to anyone, but that's part of the fun of trying to discover someone.

It's important to not use someone's own psyche against them. The intention should never be to persuade people to do something in which only you gain. Some people have more sensitive brains that are more susceptible to influence. While some people choose to remain ignorant, others legitimately don't have what it takes to grasp that they might be getting taken advantage of. You should never knowingly take advantage of another person that can't understand what's going on.

Some people require tactful approach, mostly because they aren't ready to confront their own issues. Not everyone has even a basic understanding of their brain or why it does and thinks the things it does. Some people are afraid of their own minds, so they aren't as willing to confront themselves and their emotions as other people might be. It's important to remain patient with those that might not be as self-aware as you.

Creating Vulnerability

Others respond well when one presents themselves as vulnerable. Humans connect on a societal, human, and animalistic levels. In all three of those categories, vulnerability is sought in order to make a connection. No one wants to feel as though they're talking to a refrigerator. Vulnerability is important in letting the other person know that you are human as well.

It's comforting to know there is another person that's relatable. We all have our flaws, conscious mistakes, and days when we're just lazy. Some of us have days when it can be difficult to even get out of bed. If you can show part of this side to another human, they'll be more likely to connect with you. Many of us desire to be that perfect person that's seemingly flawless. We look at those Instagram celebrities, see their perfect skin and hair, and deep down, wish that we could be like them. Most people don't realize that they wouldn't want to be friends with this person, however. There needs to be a balance when making deeper connections, so presenting yourself as too unattainable, too perfect, will only drive others away in the end.

Vulnerability is dangerous when it becomes codependency. Of course, it's good to show others that you're a real human with thoughts and feelings. However, sometimes, people become too dependent on others when trying to make a connection with them, and they end up dabbling in the dangerous world of codependency. When you get rid of your own thoughts and feelings and start to take on the opinions of others around you too much, there's a chance you might have some codependent tendencies.

There are ways that a person can present themselves as vulnerable, and they'll find that people respond well to this. Sharing too much is something that can make many people uncomfortable. You don't have to tell everyone your darkest secrets to make them think that you have a vulnerable side. There are other ways to prove to those around you that you are a relatable person that they can make a connection with.

Ask for Help

Asking for help is a way to present vulnerability.

You're letting the other person know that not only do you need them, but you're choosing to ask them for help. You're going out of your way to let them know that they have what it takes to solve your problem. You're giving another person responsibility over yourself, and that can make them feel very powerful.

It seems as though it would be counterproductive. Why would you want to show yourself as helpless to another person? The key is to not ask for too much help. You don't want to put someone else in an uncomfortable scenario where they have to do a great favor for you. Just asking for little things, to borrow something, to join you while you shop, or to house sit for a weekend, these small things can help connect you to someone you might not otherwise be able to relate to.

By creating an interaction between you and the other person, you can connect with them on a human level. You're putting more value into your relationship than if you were to keep things on a conversational level. You'll see this a lot with teachers and those that care for children. They ask the kids to do something so the children can feel important, like they have meaning. They can then connect to the adults with these small tasks. The same thinking can be carried into adulthood.

Ask for More

One way to ensure that you'll be able to persuade someone to help is by asking for more than you need in order to ensure that you'll at least get half. If you need to borrow someone's truck to help you move, ask if they can help you pack, unpack, and unload your belongings. This is a lot to ask of a person, so there's a chance they'll say no. If they do, then you could just ask to borrow their truck, the main reason you asked for help in the first place. They'll be much more likely to say yes, because they feel bad about turning down your first request.

This is a good technique that you can use in certain business negotiations. When putting an offer on a house, you're not going to offer what you actually want to pay. You'll go lower to give the other person a chance to counter back. This same kind of thinking can be applied to different interactions and moments of persuasion with other people, both on a business and personal level.

You still have to be reasonable with your requests. You can't expect to use this method to change a person. If you want more emotionally from a person, you won't be able to ask for twice as much as what you need, as everyone has their own pace. This method of persuasion isn't applicable in every scenario, but it can certainly help you in many different situations.

Making Connections

Making connections is an important part of analyzing and persuading another person. No one wants to do favors for someone they have no relationship with. No one will be able to have a genuinely happy relationship with a person that they don't feel anything for. Some people are harder to make connections with. They might have spent a good portion of their lives closed off, not wanting to meet new people. This is often because they've been hurt so often that they don't want to let themselves feel pain again. They've become an independent person that's relied on themselves and only their self for so long to provide happiness. While these people might be the most challenging to connect with, it's still possible. You have to present yourself as more vulnerable in order to let them know that you don't want to hurt them.

You can't make yourself too needy, as independent people don't like those that seem to be too reliant on other people. It's not easy to find that balance, but it is possible.

It can be hard for individuals to figure out how to even make connections. They might feel like they don't fit in, and no one understands them. Many people would be surprised to find out that there are actually many others like them that feel the same way. Even those that seemingly fit in and get along with everyone will find that they still have their moments of loneliness.

Sometimes, being a human can be incredibly lonely. You feel empty inside with your own thoughts sometimes, wondering if you can even trust and rely on yourself, let alone the people around you. This feeling of loneliness might never go away but connecting with other people can help alleviate those feelings. Letting other people know that they're not alone can also help you feel connected to others as well. There are plenty of ways to get a deeper connection with those you already know and love, but when it comes to meeting new people, there are a few methods you can use to make a connection.

Use their Name

People enjoy when you use their name. It reminds them that you're connecting to them. Bosses that can call out their employees by name are much more likely to be respected. No matter how big a company might be or how many employees there are, it's always a good idea to make sure you know as many people's names as possible. The same should be said for those that are around often. Get to know the name of your mailman, or the person that makes your coffee at Starbucks every morning.

Some people think reading the nametags of workers can be a way to connect with them, but it's always better to wait for someone to introduce themselves, or to ask them their name. Your server might have a nametag on, but instead of just calling them out, introduce yourself. People feel much more comfortable if you call them by their name, if they know your name as well.

When talking to people and having serious conversations with them, it's important to still use someone's name as well. It brings them back into the conversation and lets them know you're talking specifically about the two of you, not just generally. Many people might even realize they don't call their own spouse by their name because they've spent so much time talking *at* them and not *to* them.

Mirroring Behavior

Once you can start picking up on someone's body language, you can start to understand how to mimic their behavior. Someone that seems very confident, always standing with their arms above their heads or with them pointed out on their sides might be harder to match, but it's still important to try and mimic this behavior. Matching confidence is crucial, especially in a deal where you're trying to persuade the other person.

You don't want to do this to be manipulative, but rather, to make them feel comfortable. Some people might notice that a person is feeling particularly uncomfortable, so they might take advantage of this and exert their confidence and power over the other person. This should never be done, as you're closing off the opportunity for them to open up to you.

If you notice someone is uncomfortable and closed off, reduce your confidence level to match. It lets them know that they can trust you and depend on you. If someone is picking at their fingers and rapidly tapping their feet out of anxiety, you don't have to do the same. Just make sure that you're at their level or lower, whether that means you have to sit or stand. Then keep your arms relaxed, maybe tilting your head to let them know that you're listening and ready to hear what they have to say. You don't want to make anyone feel more uncomfortable than they already are.

Flattery gets you everywhere

Sometimes, sucking up to someone can really work. You don't want to be inauthentic or too over the top with what compliments you're giving to another person, but it's still important to remember just how much a little extra love can go. There's a chance you're already thinking the things you want to say anyway, so why not tell them how you feel, as long as it's positive.

Flattery doesn't just have to be telling someone how gorgeous or smart they are. It can be as simple as picking up their favorite snack when you're at the store or remembering to ask how their vacation went if you know they went away for the weekend. Some people might see these things as "kissing ass," or "brown nosing," but trying to make a positive connection should be part of our everyday life.

Even if someone sees what you're doing, they're still appreciative of your conscious effort to make a connection. It can be pretty obvious in some instances that a person is trying to flatter you, especially if they're normally closed off or seemingly careless. While some people can be bothered by this, most will still appreciate the effort you're putting into trying to make a connection with them.

The Power of Words

You, because, free, instantly, and new, these are the most powerful words in the English language. "You," is an important word, because people love hearing about themselves. Listen to a 1-3-year-old talk next time you're around them. "Me," and "mine," are likely going to be a huge part of their vocabulary. It might even be the first word most people learn!

"Because," is an important word, because many people are looking for an explanation. In a word with so many curiosities and possibilities, we can feel overwhelmed with how little we know. Humans are obsessed with labels, and most people like to know the reason behind something. When they hear the word "because," their brain kicks on and becomes more alert, waiting for the explanation they're so desperately seeking.

"Free" is a popular word, for many reasons in our society. On one hand, it means free stuff! People will spend three hundred dollars on something they don't need if it means they get one small FREE gift to go along with that. You can really hypnotize someone by using the word "free."

"Free," is also an important word because so many people desire freedom and independence in their lives. Even the most codependent people like to hear the word "free," even if it's just them getting an illusion of what freedom might mean.

"Instantly," is a great word because so many people are obsessed with time. We all have to face the dark truth: we're going to die one day. Even those that are in their 20s still have to know that their days are numbered. We try to fight change as much as possible, but time is unbeatable, so when we can get more of it, we're hooked, someone promising something instant is going to be popular.

"New," is the last of the five most popular words. As humans, our brains are wired to constantly look for new growth. Some people might be afraid of change, but we still look for new things. "New," represents growth and life at the same time. Some people might want to wear the same shirt they've had for years versus a brand new one. Still, if offered a new or an old sandwich, they're going to go for the new one.

These five words are very important to include in everyone's vocabulary, whether you're trying to persuade someone or not.

What you do with your body is important, but the words that you decide to share are crucial as well. It's important to remember not only with what you're saying, but with what others are speaking as well. Not everything that is said is exactly what is meant.

Psychological Theories

Most of us learned in early elementary school what a scientific theory was. It usually involved the idea of someone who then tests that theory to see if what they believed is right. A psychological theory is similar, in that a psychiatrist or psychologist thought of something they saw among their patients, decided to test their theory, and then got differing results. There are numerous psychological theories that are important, and the more you know, the better you'll be able to analyze someone else.

There is a lot to know about different psychology aspects in order to understand all of the psychological theories the world of science has to offer. Not everyone has to be a therapist or psychiatrist to understand what some different psychological theories might be.

You should try coming up with your own as well. Maybe you noticed a behavior among a group of people that you interact with. What is the root cause for them reacting this way? How might they react differently to a certain stimulus versus another group of people? Everyone is different, so not every theory is going to apply. It's still very interesting to see how often you can be right about the psychological predictions that you're making.

If you can't think of any of your own theories to test, we've put together three that seem to be very popular and accurate among most people and the way that you can analyze those around you. These are important theories in making connections with other people, as well as persuading them should you have to in a certain scenario.

Priming

If you think of priming, you might commonly associate the term with painting. You pick out a primer to put on the walls before you decide to paint. This will ensure that the ugly mustard yellow the walls were painted before won't show through as you put a new coat of baby blue on. In psychological terms, priming is very similar to this idea.

This involves setting up conversations and actions for future preparation. This idea is most important in negotiations or moments of persuasion. Priming involves slipping words, images, and ideas into conversations before confronting the actual thing. Priming is used for people that don't like surprises, or those that aren't as willing to change.

Picture a husband and wife. Maybe the wife wants to have kids, but she isn't so sure her husband is ready. She knows that he reacts poorly to change and that when confronted, he tends to close himself off. It took her five years to get him to propose, so she needs to be careful about bringing up the baby conversation. She might start priming him by first putting on a movie about a baby. Maybe she'll make small comments here and there about wanting a baby or take detours through the baby sections at the local department stores. She'll want to prime him for the baby conversation, so he doesn't run and hide once she finally brings it up.

This type of behavior can be rather manipulative if not used for the right reasons. If the woman's husband had stated over and over again that he did not want children and never would change his mind, she shouldn't be priming him. However, there are some people that need a psychological push, and scaring the husband away wouldn't be the way to do so. The way that this behavior would be negatively manipulative is if someone is using it for personal gain only. If the change, or what is being primed, is going to benefit both parties, then it can be a useful tool in order to get what you want.

Amplification Hypothesis

The amplification hypothesis is one that involves heightening the excitement or negativity surrounding a certain subject. Many people probably use this sort of process without even realizing they are doing so. The process involves taking a subject, item, or other idea, and basically gassing it up, making it seem more exciting, and amplifying it to the next level. This involves either talking something down or building it up in order to alter perspectives.

Let's look at the husband and wife from the last section. She might decide to use this process by talking about how great babies are. Maybe she'll come home and discuss her friends' baby and how cute and perfect it was. She certainly won't mention that she still has puke on her shirt and instead only talk about the adorable noises and faces the baby made. Alternatively, the husband might amplify his hatred for children, if that's how he really feels. Maybe he'll point out a crying baby when they're in public, saying things like, "thank God we don't have kids."

The amplification hypothesis is usually true, but to use it isn't always the best option. Sometimes, it's better to just be honest about one's feelings and have a normal discussion without hidden meanings. This type of process can still be helpful for those that can't discuss things as openly as they'd like. When working on different projects in business or in your personal life, if you're working with others, there are going to be some group decisions that have to made. Sometimes, the amplification process can help you show your feelings without directly breaking down someone else's idea or saying anything that might hurt or offend another person.

The Scarcity Effect

The scarcity effect is the idea that when there is less of something, it can become more desirable. This is mostly thought of in sales. Think of the last store you went to. There were likely advertisements that said things like, "only two days left," "while supplies last," or "limited time only." Most of the time, this isn't true at all and are phrases only used to get people to buy quicker. This effect seriously works which is why so many businesses still use it. The same kind of effect can be made in different conversations and relationships. When trying to persuade someone, limiting the time or availability of an option can help sway them quicker.

Playing hard to get can help. While it's important to show vulnerability to others in order to make deeper connections, it's also important to maintain a certain distance. There's an idea that some people like "bad boys," and this is related to the scarcity effect. The idea that you can't have something makes people want it even more. The fear of regret that comes along with not getting something can be what drives a person to make a decision.

Think of a jar of cookies. If there are two jars, one completely filled and one with only three or four cookies left, most will go for the jar that's almost empty. They could be the same type of cookie, but most will assume that the jar that's almost empty has better tasting cookies. More people put their time and effort into eating the other cookies, so they probably have something better to offer.

Chapter 3 – Subliminal Persuasion

The idea of subliminal persuasion involves convincing someone to do something below their conscious level. You wouldn't blatantly persuade someone if you're being subliminal about it. Instead, you would try to convince them to do what you want without them even realizing what you're doing.

The idea of subliminal persuasion is mostly thought of in advertising. There are many companies that will do whatever they can to convince us to buy something, even if it means partially brainwashing us. The idea of subliminal persuasion doesn't have to be so insidious for those that wish to use these tactics to help persuade another person.

There are many important parts of subliminally persuading someone. You'll first want to make sure that you're doing it for the right reasons. You don't want to become someone that brainwashes others. It's not about getting into their head and tricking them into thinking something. Instead, you should be looking at what you know about them and using this in your plan for persuasion.

It's Not about Manipulation

You never want to make a person feel like they are crazy. You don't want to give sneaky hints that will make them question their own sanity. Subliminal persuasion should just be used as a nice way to tell someone how you really feel when you might be too scared to say the blatant truth.

Some people just have a harder time accepting truth, persuasion, or reality than others. These types of people can't be blatantly told what someone else wants. Sometimes, people like to disagree with others just for the sake of being controversial. There are ways that you can take around obviously asking someone for something.

Subliminal persuasion should never be about manipulation. You shouldn't be "tricking" someone into something that will only benefit you. You should be using this method to try and better prevent against being subliminally persuaded yourself. It's also helpful for stubborn, intimidating, or other types of people that can't be so easily conversed with.

Confidence is Key

The trick to subliminally persuading someone is to exude as much confidence as possible. There are some people that will see overt confidence as delusional, so you don't want to take it too far. However, no one is going to be persuaded, no matter how subliminal you get, by someone that can't even stand up for their own thoughts and opinions.

Confidence is also important in order to distract

the person from realizing that you might be trying to persuade them of something. Picture talking to your mom or dad, hoping to get to borrow the car again when you were a teenager. You would want to use some confidence, but not so much that you would want them to think you don't care about their permission. In order to subliminally persuade them, you might bring up the fact that there's no one else that can safely drive you to a party. Instead of blatantly asking and giving them the option to say no, instead, you're more able to sway them to your form of thinking. It can then become their own idea to let you borrow the car for the weekend.

Body Language Techniques

In the first chapter, many different body language theories were discussed, giving you insight into how or why someone uses their body in the way that they do. Using these same techniques is also important when it comes to subliminal persuasion. You'll want to show confidence, while also maintaining vulnerability, when trying to subliminally persuade someone.

Keep Speech Clear

An important part of subliminal persuasion is to actually speak clearly about what you want. Some people can be tricked if you speak quickly or use confusing words that they don't understand. This isn't fair and can be a form of negative manipulation.

Instead of trying to trick someone into giving you what you want, you can do it in a fair way that doesn't require confusing them. Plan out what you have to say if you must, but not too much. You don't want the conversation to feel like you're being too formal. Instead, pick out a few key points you feel are necessary, as well as some important words that you want to put emphasis on in your speech.

If someone can see that you're speaking with diction and confidence, they'll be more likely to agree to what you're asking than if you just trick them into saying yes by using confusing and jumbled language. That way, if something goes wrong later after the deal is made, you can remind them that you laid out the terms very clearly before they agreed.

Framing Conversations

Like we mentioned in the previous section, it can be incredibly helpful to lay out the framework for the conversations that you'll be having with others. You never want to write down exactly what you're going to say, as this will come off very static and obviously practiced. No one wants to respond well or say "yes" compassionately to a robot.

Framing is important because it helps build the foundation of your persuasion. You'll want to write down what your goals are, and how you're going to go about achieving those. It's also important to include the bumps and consequences you might face so you can properly prepare for those as well.

Choose Positivity

It can be hard to remain positive, especially when trying to persuade someone of something serious. Positivity almost always works better than using negativity, however. Frame your requests using positive words rather than negative ones. If you have to ask your parents to borrow $1,000, it can be nerve-wracking. Instead of using a negative explanation, such as, "I just lost my job and I'm behind on all my bills and don't know how I'm going to catch up," try being more positive, such as, "I only need $1000 because I'm in between jobs, but I applied to several new positions and know that the $1,000 is all I need to make sure I don't get behind!"

While both situations are tricky, your parents are going to see that they won't have as much risk with the second phrasing that they might face from the first scenario. It's the same situation. You're unemployed and you need money. However, you found the positivity in the second phrasing, showing your parents the hopefulness of the scenario as well. This is applicable in more ways than just asking someone for money.

Get people to start saying yes more. Instead of asking someone, "When are we going to set a date for the wedding?" try asking, "How does November first sound?" Instead of giving them the option to blow off the conversation, they have to confront the issue head-on. Don't give someone the option to avoid the conversation. Instead, think of a yes or no question that you can ask that can start leading the conversation.

Another example would be asking your roommate to have a party. You wouldn't want to say, "Can I have a party tomorrow?" This gives them the option to say no. Instead, try saying, "How about we have a party tomorrow night and then Sunday we can spend all day cleaning and relaxing." This puts the idea of the whole picture in their head so they're more likely to say yes, instead of making them confront an idea they might want to instantly say no to.

Plan Your Outcome

When writing a story, it's always best to think of the beginning, the middle, and the end, before you go on with writing the book. This way, you can include things in the beginning that might lead to hints as to what's going to happen in the end. How many times have you watched a movie, only to realize there were clues to who the murderer was all along!

This kind of planning is important to have in certain conversations as well. If you can plan what you want to gain from a specific interaction, you can include hints to that in the beginning of the conversation. This is an important way to prime as well as lay the framework for whatever your argument might be.

Physical Persuasion

How you physically look can be very persuasive for another person. Not everyone is physically large, so they might feel as though they can't stand up to others. It can be challenging to be a small person that has to stand up to those that are bigger!

At the same time, some people that are larger might feel like they have difficulty being vulnerable. They might feel as though all people see is their size, not giving them a chance thinking that they might be too tough or mean to approach.

There are ways around our own physical appearance that can help persuade other people. Even if someone is very large, they can still have meaningful connections not based around fear.

Those that are smaller than most can still have a loud voice to help them stand up for themselves when they need to.

Choosing What to Wear

As much as most might not like to admit it, it can be important what we choose to wear, especially when making negotiations. The first step in choosing what is right to wear is to make sure that it's something you're comfortable in. This doesn't always mean sweatpants, but something that at least aligns with your personal style and clothing that you would actually be seen in. Others can tell when you might not be wearing something you would otherwise. A suit can look like a costume on someone that's normally in button-down shirts and slacks.

The next step is to make sure that it appropriately matches the occasion. Some people want to get as dressed up as possible, thinking their finest jewels and nicest threads will make them look better than most. You still want to make sure you're not overdoing it so that you can be approachable.

Color and patterns are important to consider as well. Warm colors can be inviting, but something that's too bold of a shade of red or yellow might also be a signal to be cautious for the other person. Blue and green can be welcoming colors as well, but you don't want to look like the ice king in too much baby blue. How someone responds to a color could be a direct indication of how they'll respond to your persuasion.

Scent is Important

Scent is much more persuasive than many people would think. There are some department stores that even release Christmas smelling scents around the holidays in order to elicit a happier mood that will cause people to spend more money!

When choosing a scent, it's important to wear

something that matches your natural body scent. The samples you see for perfume at the store aren't just so you can smell the product. It's also so you can try the scent out for a day and see how it mixes with the aromas you naturally give off. Perfume can be expensive but look at it as an investment towards persuasion and not just something that will make you smell nice.

NLP Tactics

NLP stands for neuro-linguistic programming. The idea is to look at the neurology, linguistics, and programming of a person to help determine what it is about them that makes them a unique individual.

Everyone has their own version of reality based around the way they were raised as well as the things they like. Once that reality is created, it can become a formula for how they handle different scenarios. NLP is discussed more in book one, so by this point, you should have a basic understanding of what it means.

Once you become aware of how someone else might be using NLP tactics on you, you can also use those tactics on other people as well.

Switching Up Physiology

Sometimes, switching up your physical space might be the exact thing that you need in order to use NLP to persuade or analyze another person. Maybe there's something blocking your way during the conversation. You might consider actually moving both you and the person you're talking to in order to create a more welcoming environment. If you feel like the conversation isn't going where you wanted, maybe take a bathroom break and give the person some time alone.

If you come back from the bathroom and things still are the same, suggest switching up the location. Maybe you could go for a walk or step out onto the patio. Sometimes, you don't always have to go this far. Perhaps just shifting your body movement or the way you're sitting is enough to re-engage the other person.

Visualization

Visualization is a great way for some people to achieve their goals. There are so many things that might seem out of reach, but you'd be surprised at how much you can accomplish if you just visualize what you want.

It can start by speaking something into existence. If you want to move to L.A. to become an actress, start talking about it. Don't tell people that you just want to do it at some point. Actually, say you're going to do it, and you'll be surprised at how much you can influence yourself towards these goals.

Write it down if you have to as well. This is more

a method of self-persuasion than one that you can use on others, but it still certainly helps to speak and write about the goals and wishes you want to see fulfilled.

Taking Away the Ability to Say No

We briefly touched on this earlier but taking away the ability for another person to say no is an NLP tactic you can use for persuasion. Instead of saying, "Do you want to go out to dinner tonight?" ask someone, "Where are we going to dinner tonight?" You haven't given them the option to say no to your dinner date. They might say they can't anyway, but at least you tried to take away that option.

Instead of saying, "Can I have one?" say, "How many can I have?" Most people won't even realize that you've taken away their ability to turn you down.

Conclusion

This book should have provided you with a basic understanding of how to analyze and persuade those around you. While every individual is unique in their own way, there are certainly things that are similar between each and every person. Most of us have a desire to fulfill our own needs and wants, and when those ideas are realized, the person can be better analyzed. How a person was raised and the environment that they grew up in is very important in determining what it is that makes a person unique.

When analyzing another person, it starts with looking at their body language. Do they hold themselves high or do they hide behind their own body? How a person uses their eyes, face, and arms, are the most important parts of determining what they might really be like. You can realize that someone who seems confident might actually be debilitated by their anxiety if you start to notice the way they hold themselves.

You could also discover that someone you thought you could trust is actually deceiving you.

It can be hard to pinpoint what it is about a person that separates them from others, and why they might act the way they do. You'll never have a complete understanding of another person, but you will at least be able to start to realize why they might act the way they do.

Once you've been able to analyze someone, you can then start to persuade them. This is important in some cases to get what you want, or at the very least, get what you deserve. Just as we discussed in book one, you can read this over and over again, but unless you take action, nothing is going to change. It can be hard to start to become aware of yourself, but it's a key step in becoming aware of those around you.

Once you have the ability to analyze yourself and others, you'll be able to better persuade and convince them as well. When you can do this, you'll realize all the power you have over your own life.

How to Analyze People: Dark Psychology

Thank you!

Before you go, I just wanted to say thank you for purchasing my book.

You could have picked from dozens of other books on the same topic but you took a chance and chose this one.

So, a HUGE thanks to you for getting this book and for reading all the way to the end.

Now I wanted to ask you for a small favor. **Could you please consider posting a review on the platform? Reviews are one of the easiest ways to support the work of independent authors.**

This feedback will help me continue to write the type of books that will help you get the results you want. So if you enjoyed it, please let me know! (-:

www.ingramcontent.com/pod-product-compliance
Lightning Source LLC
Chambersburg PA
CBHW071725020426
42333CB00017B/2390